THE TEACHERS' GLOSSARY
TO RECOVERY

THE TEACHERS' GLOSSARY TO RECOVERY

HOW WE GOT FROM AA TO Z

Michele Leigh Dionisio and Tricia N. Ragusa

This book is not intended as a substitute for medical advice. The reader should regularly consult a physician in matters relating to his/her health and particularly with respect to any symptoms that may require diagnosis or medical attention.

(health, alternative healing)

ISBN: 197469335X
ISBN 13: 9781974693351

DEDICATION

To our earth angel and spiritual teacher, Corrina Dileo, who got us connected, kept us on track, and inspired a true love of the divine within us.

To our A-team on the other side, who gently pushed us, protected us, and guided us this year. We honor and love you all very much.

Roy Ragusa
Margaret Gioello
Grace Crocitto
Elaine Kennedy Dionisio
Michelina Gioello
Kate Rose Eichin

To our mothers, Susan Ragusa and Donnamarie Dionisio, who, at our darkest moments, never gave up on us, never lost faith, and showed us how powerful unconditional love really is. We are better mothers to our own children because of you.

We are here to give you **HUGS.**
Find your **HUGS** through the use of this glossary.

This glossary is a book on how to recover from life. Together, as a **Starfish Tribe** of men, women, children and adolescents, we recover from substance abuse, sex addiction, love addiction, food addiction, shopping addiction, and any other addiction with which you are attempting to fill a hole.

What are you looking for? You are looking to be whole. We all are. To find yourself in your purest form, you must first find what we like to call your HUGS. Your HUGS is your **higher power,** whether it is the **universe**, **God**, or your own **spirit**. Anything that is bigger than you can give you all the HUGS you need to become the best version of you. In finding your HUGS, you begin a journey of healing. When healing takes place we recover from mental health struggles, trauma, grief, divorce, toxic relationships, codependency, postpartum depression and many other hardships in life.

Join us in our movement to wholeness. Join us in recovery. Join us in finding your HUGS and your soul's purpose, and begin to contribute to helping the divine purpose of the universe to naturally evolve.

HOW TO USE THIS GLOSSARY

WE ARE TEACHERS. We like direct, explicit instructions. Here are some suggestions on how to use this book.

Each letter of the alphabet represents an idea, strategy, or concept for entering into and remaining in a recovered state. So, you could:

Read **one letter per day**, and consider this a **twenty-seven-day** journey to enlightenment.

You can read the content in the order it appears, begin from the very end, or start right in the middle. Read in whatever way you feel drawn to.

You can take three deep breaths and ask your HUGS what you need to see, and then randomly turn to a page.

You could read from beginning to end, as you would any other book.

You could focus on one entry at a time and become an expert in that particular practice.

However you choose to use this glossary, what we do know is this: this book is living and breathing; the divine inspired us in writing it; and we believe we are simply vessels. Therefore, whenever you pick this book up, you will be guided by your HUGS to see and get exactly what you need in that moment. Your HUGS will speak to you through this text. Each time you read with us, you are reading with the divine, so you will get something new—always, without fail. Finally, we suggest you take what you love and leave the rest behind. Our hope is that at least one entry, if not more, in this book can become the door to finding your HUGS and discovering your life's true purpose.

CONTENTS

A a

ALCOHOLICS ANONYMOUS
THE 12 STEPS

MANY PEOPLE SEEKING recovery from substance abuse or traumatic life events typically find themselves in a support group of some type or a twelve-step program. Most people do not realize that Alcoholics Anonymous (AA) is simply a textbook that's also known as the "Big Book." What comes from that text are the widely recognized twelve steps, and these steps can be used to overcome anything life brings to us. Addictions or obsessions of the mind have nothing to do with the substance or the obsession itself. It is the person who needs to change. There is no arguing that the twelve-step process, which was born in AA, provide people with a path to look inward. Many who have gone through the steps are able to change old behaviors and patterns, clean up their pasts, and experience the psychic change necessary to recover from literally anything. Recovering people are similar to the lotus flower of Buddhism. We begin with a life of mud and mess, but as we trust the process of the twelve steps, we emerge from the mud as a beautiful flower ready to experience a new life of love and light.

Ask Yourself: Am I willing to consider that it is *me* who needs to change?

Our Experience: The twelve steps have transformed us from the people we once were and have since given us a blueprint for living a spiritually fit, recovered, and joyful life.

Prayer: HUGS, please grant me the willingness to understand that I am the problem. Allow me to be open to the process of true change.

Positive Affirmation: I will be open to the process of the twelve steps and be astonished by the outcome.

Words to Live By: "Just like the lotus flower, trust in the light, grow through the mud, and believe in the new."

THROUGHOUT YOUR DAY

We found that the following has worked for us.

MORNING

Upon awakening, set your intention to do the "right" thing throughout the day. We all know the difference between what is right and wrong. The simple mantra of the steps is "Do the next right thing."

NOON

When faced with decisions, always pause, think, ask for guidance, and react with love. Putting love out attracts love in. We live by the saying, "Would you rather be right or happy?" The universe rewards those who live by its laws.

NIGHT

Review your day honestly. Look at where you did the right thing and reacted to people and situations with loving kindness. Always examine *your* part in things. Remember, we can only be responsible for ourselves. In situations where you believe you did wrong, immediately take responsibility and consider what you must do differently next time to respond with love. Remember: "Progress, not perfection."

Date:

Notes

_____

_____

_____

_____

_____

_____

_____

_____

_____

_____

_____

_____

_____

_____

_____

_____

_____

_____

_____

_____

_____

_____

Date:

Notes

_____

_____

_____

_____

_____

_____

_____

_____

_____

_____

_____

_____

_____

_____

_____

_____

_____

_____

_____

_____

_____

_____

A a

ATTITUDE

RECOVERY IS NOT easy. If we said it was, we would be lying. We encounter highs and lows each day and in every aspect of life. Attitude is one of the most important factors in how we cope with what comes our way. A positive attitude will ultimately determine how each day turns out. When thinking about your attitude, understand that you really only have two options. You can walk through your challenges in life with an attitude of self-pity and misery, or you can walk in gratitude and focus on your blessings, no matter how bad your situation seems. Your life is a reflection of your thoughts and attitude. If you are unhappy with any aspect of your life, it makes sense to first examine your attitude.

Ask Yourself: Am I willing to consider that my attitude is drastically affecting my wellbeing?

Our Experience: We did not enter into recovery and then suddenly experience perfect lives. The truth is, life is hard. However, your attitude in every situation will drastically affect the outcome. When we improved our attitudes and outlook, our lives improved as well.

Prayer: HUGS, please allow me to have a positive attitude and outlook toward life.

Positive Affirmation: I am too positive to be doubtful, too optimistic to be fearful, too determined to be defeated, and too blessed to be stressed.

Words to Live By: "The only disability in life is a bad attitude." —Scott Hamilton

THROUGHOUT YOUR DAY
We found that the following has worked for us.

MORNING
Set your intention to only use positive words when thinking and speaking about yourself, others, and situations. Visualize your circumstance or situation as positively as you can (the glass is either half-full or half-empty). Which vision will you feed today?

NOON
Use words that evoke strength and success. Fill your mind with thoughts and words that make you feel strong and happy. Tell yourself throughout the day that you are safe, you are loved, and you are strong.

NIGHT

Honestly analyze what went wrong and why. More specifically, see where attitude caused you trouble, and be willing to strive for a more positive outlook in similar situations in the future. With consistent practice of this new attitude, it will become second nature to you. In a short time, you will see how far you have come.

Other *A* Entries

Acupuncture: This traditional form of Chinese medicine is most commonly used to treat pain. Needles inserted into certain areas of the body can help to rebalance your Chi or life energy. This alternative form of medicine can also be used to treat addiction, depression, anxiety, and many physical ailments and can promote an overall sense of wellbeing.

Angels: We believe that the universe or God speaks to us through other people with the hope of sending us signs or messages. Connection and relationships with others are an essential part of a spiritual awakening. On this journey, the people around you (often those you randomly encounter) can quite literally be Earth Angels. If this is of special interest to you, read *The Celestine Prophecy* by James Redfield; you will not be sorry you did.

Animal Therapy: Animal therapy is a type of therapy that uses animals as a form of treatment. The goal is to improve social, emotional, and cognitive functioning. Many people in recovery find their purpose in working with animals.

Art Therapy: Art therapy is a form of psychotherapy that inhibits free self-expression through various forms of art. Many people find their purpose in recovery through art, and art therapy is a great way to begin that journey.

Awareness: Develop an awareness of your habits, actions, patterns, and thoughts. Also be aware of how your actions affect others. Awareness is the first step to change. In waking up, you become an objective observer of your own life and more conscious of your thoughts.

Date:

Notes

Date:

Notes

_____

_____

_____

_____

_____

_____

_____

_____

_____

_____

_____

_____

_____

_____

_____

_____

_____

_____

_____

_____

_____

_____

_____

B b

BREATHE

CONSIDER THIS: BREATHING is the first thing we do when we are born and the very last thing we do before we die. This fact alone points to the importance of breathing. When we get upset, people tell us to breathe. Why? Because breath is the essence of life. It immediately brings us back to our center, improves our focus, and reconnects us to the energy we need to conquer anything we encounter. Breath is life giving and the simplest way to connect with a source of power that is greater than us. There are many different types of breathing practices that can be used to create an overall sense of wellbeing and even euphoria. Some well-known techniques include stimulating breath, also known as bellows breath, 4-7-8 breath, and breath counting. We must all remember that breathing is free and that we can stop at any time and any place to breathe.

Ask Yourself: Am I willing to consider some simple breathing techniques that may prove to be life changing?

Our Experience: In stressful situations, we have learned to pause instead of reacting. We focus on a technique of using our breath to center and ground ourselves before proceeding. By returning to our breath, it can give us a new perspective on any situation, and it also helps reduce the amount of fear that inherently comes from stress.

Prayer: HUGS, grant me the willingness to try new breathing techniques and to know that the life-giving qualities of breath will transform me.

Positive Affirmation: I am whole and healing with every breath I take.

Words to Live By: "When you own your breath, nobody can steal your peace."
—Unknown

THROUGHOUT YOUR DAY
We found that the following has worked for us.

MORNING
Begin your day with the following breathing practice. Sit up and feel the earth beneath you. This can be on the floor in your bedroom, on a yoga mat, outdoors, or even in your bed. Breathe in the love of the universe for four seconds and visualize yourself surrounded by light. Breathe out the idea of trying to control everything for four seconds. Repeat this process three times or as many times as you need to.

Noon

When faced with a stressful situation, return to long, deep breathing or any technique that has worked for you until the negative or anxious feelings have passed. We have found that different breathing techniques work at different times and for different stressors. Try them all!

Night

Before going to sleep, try the following:

Exhale through your mouth.
Breathe in for a count of **five**.
Suspend the breath for a count of **five**.
Exhale for a count of **seven**.
Repeat this **three** times.
Find whatever technique works for you—the key is consistency.

Other *B* Entries

Baths: Baths are an excellent way to relax. Epsom salt baths are especially beneficial in reducing inflammations and detoxing the body of impurities. We just can't help but to relax in warm water, laying in a horizontal position. Baths can also relieve skin irritations and help with sore or tense muscles. They help with sleep disturbances and reduce pain and anxiety. To make your bath a little extra special, try using a bath bomb, essential oils, or candles, reading a good book, or just playing relaxing music.

Binaural Beats Meditation: Regular meditation is helpful in reducing stress. However, for some people, meditation is stress producing because they struggle to quiet their minds. Binaural beats meditation induces a meditative state through listening to certain repetitive sound patterns. The tones get a person to a meditative state quickly and effectively. For more information, go to www.binauralbeats.com.

Bloggers: There are a multitude of extremely talented bloggers on the Internet who write about various topics in recovery. Chances are, whatever you are recovering from, there is someone writing about it, and if not, you can start your own blog. Bloggers become experts in their fields, write from personal experiences, and can offer advice on many topics. You can also build a support network and interact with new people who are working toward similar goals.

Blogging: To us, blogging is a form of therapy. Writing about your experiences not only helps others but will also help you; writing is said to be one of the most therapeutic practices in recovery. Writing in recovery can help you build a support network and an audience that allow you to share your personal experiences and to learn from others. Writing in recovery is not so much about the end product as it is the process of expression that leads to healing. In addition, many people in recovery, ourselves included, found our purpose in writing.

Breath of Starfish: Breath of Starfish is a five-finger meditation that can be used as both a meditation and breathing technique. Make a starfish with one hand by spreading your five fingers out wide. Then, using the pointer finger on the opposite hand, trace the starfish one finger at a time. As you do this, count a long inhale and exhale as one and the next as two. Repeat this process five times until you have covered the whole starfish.

Date:

Notes

_____

_____

_____

_____

_____

_____

_____

_____

_____

_____

_____

_____

_____

_____

_____

_____

_____

_____

_____

_____

_____

_____

_____

_____

Date:

Notes

C c

COPING SKILLS

In RECOVERY, IT is essential to establish a variety of coping skills. For many people in recovery, alcohol, drugs, food, or any other unhealthy obsession was the solution to life's problems. Since we are looking to extinguish that behavior and/or substance as our solution, we need to have something substituted in its place when we're faced with adversity; we must have a healthy coping mechanism or skill. It takes practice and consistency to develop these skills. However, these skills do become habitual when used over time. For example, recognizing what we can and cannot control is an important coping skill. We also suggest slowing down, pausing, breathing, and thinking before acting or speaking. Practicing mindfulness, exercising, avoiding triggers (HALT—hungry, angry, lonely, tired), attending therapy (either individual or group), journaling, and meditating are all healthy ways to cope with the stresses of life.

Ask Yourself: Am I willing to establish a new set of coping skills?

Our Experience: Practice and consistency are the most important aspects of developing a habitual set of coping skills. You will make mistakes and revert to old ways from time to time. Do not condemn yourself—just try again next time.

Prayer: HUGS, please allow me the willingness to develop new ways of coping with life.

Positive Affirmation: I can learn a new way to cope with whatever life gives me.

Words to Live By: "Peace is not the absence of conflict but the ability to cope with it." —Ronald Regan

THROUGHOUT YOUR DAY

We found that the following has worked for us.

MORNING
Set your intention to focus on one of the above-mentioned coping skills.

NOON
Practice that skill throughout the day, and know that you may need to use several at any given time.

NIGHT
Evaluate the different methods you used that day to cope. Journaling can be very helpful in determining

which coping skills work best for you and which were ineffective. If you have peace in your mind and heart when you handled situations in this new way, you will develop a sense of pride you never had before. Many people are shocked when they realize something as simple as a breathing technique or a daily meditation can change their attitude and perceptions when it comes to difficult situations or life events. Some coping skills will work for you, and some simply will not. This is trial and error here. There are many excellent resources on the web that list various coping skills.

Other *C* Entries

Candles: Candles are great for relaxing and making your home look tranquil and peaceful. Certain scents, such as lavender and certain berries, can help with relaxation. They add color, a warm glow, and an overall softness to your surroundings.

Chakras: Chakras are the energy centers of our bodies. Blocked chakras can lead to various health-related issues, so it is important to keep this energy flowing freely. Opening, balancing, and healing your chakras can lead to a spiritual awakening and allow a person to feel fully alive. There are many great books written for beginners that explain the different chakras and the benefits.

Cooking: Cooking can be used as a form of therapy. The process of cooking helps with mindfulness and creativity. It is also a relaxing activity (if you like it) that is linked to eating, which can feel like a reward and bring you and your loved ones joy in the process.

Crystals: Crystal healing therapy involves placing stones on the body to draw out negative energies. It is an alternative medicine technique that can cure certain ailments and protect the body against disease and illness. Crystals can also be used to aid in establishing and maintaining a meditation practice.

Date:

Notes

Date:

Notes

_____

_____

_____

_____

_____

_____

_____

_____

_____

_____

_____

_____

_____

_____

_____

_____

_____

_____

_____

_____

_____

_____

_____

_____

D d

DANIEL DIET

THROUGHOUT THIS JOURNEY, we have learned that what you eat directly affects the way you think, feel, act, and respond. They say in recovery to live by the acronym HALT, remembering to never get too hungry, angry, lonely, or tired. Not getting too hungry is essential, but we've also noticed that the foods you take in can directly affect your connection to spirit. The Daniel Diet, which was inspired by the biblical prophet Daniel, is a way to eat healthily while also obtaining closeness to your HUGS. Daniel himself often fasted, eating fruits, vegetables, and water to set himself apart for God. However, fasting is not the only idea to come out of this biblical diet. It is a way of eating that can keep you healthy, give you energy, and enhance spirituality. The Daniel Diet is based on a vegan diet that promotes healthy eating while greatly enhancing the connection of the mind, body, and spirit. In addition to the Daniel Diet, there are many healthy eating plans that can aid in an overall sense of wellbeing and that can give your body the fuel it needs for maximum performance. Some of these plans include the Whole30,

Mediterranean diet, DASH diet, Paleolithic diet, South Beach diet, and the Zone diet, to name a few.

Ask Yourself: Am I willing to try a healthier eating plan as a means of enhancing my mind, body, and spirit connection?

Our Experience: Not only does this diet help you to lose weight fast, but it also enhances the balance between the body, mind, and spirit. While following this eating plan, we found we had far more energy and experienced a feeling of overall wellbeing.

Prayer: HUGS, allow me the willingness to look at my diet and consider eating differently.

Positive Affirmation: I will eat foods that are healthy for my mind, body, and spirit.

Words to Live By: "Love yourself enough to live a healthy lifestyle."

THROUGHOUT YOUR DAY
We found that the following has worked for us.

Morning
Set your intention to stick to healthy eating for the day, and plan to write everything down that you eat. Be sure

to chew your food slowly and develop good eating habits. This can be something as simple as sitting while you are eating (the moms of young children can relate to that one).

NOON

Mindfully eat throughout the day. Pay attention to what you put in your body. Focus on fruits and vegetables, and drink plenty of water.

NIGHT

Notice the difference in the way you feel after a day of being committed to healthy eating. Review the foods you ate during the day, and commit to another day of the same eating routine. It is also beneficial to weigh yourself and take your measurements prior to a healthy-eating lifestyle change.

For more information, visit www.daniel-fast.com.

Other *D* Entries

Dance: We cannot stress this one enough; we hope you dance! You can do this alone in your room or out with friends. Many styles of dance provide various benefits. Dance can help people express themselves, improve confidence, and boost self-esteem. It encourages imagination and taps into our creative energies. It is also a great exercise that is tons of fun and excellent for your physical and mental wellbeing. We may be biased with this one because we love to dance.

Debtors Anonymous: Many people entering the world of recovery find that their financial situations are rather dismal. This twelve-step fellowship has a phenomenal system for organizing, tackling, and getting out of debt. Many people use this fellowship and not only recover financially but end up thriving.

Dialectical Behavior Therapy (DBT): This is a therapy used to treat mood disorders and change unhelpful patterns of behavior. DBT focuses on awareness and mindfulness along with techniques derived from meditative practice.

Date:

Notes

Date:

Notes

_____

_____

_____

_____

_____

_____

_____

_____

_____

_____

_____

_____

_____

_____

_____

_____

_____

_____

_____

_____

_____

_____

_____

_____

E e

EXERCISE

Body. Mind. Spirit. Do not think for one second that they are disconnected. If one is left out of your self-care routine, they will all be out of alignment. We must learn to take care of all three in order to be whole and to feel our best. Caring for our physical vessel that was given to us is of utmost importance, and exercise is a great way to do it. For people in recovery, exercise is essential because it decreases nervous, anxious energy while increasing dopamine naturally. Although most of the work done by those in recovery is an inside job, let's face it—when we look good on the outside, we tend to feel better on the inside. There is no arguing that exercise can help to enhance our physical appearance while simultaneously improving our overall health and wellbeing.

Ask Yourself: Am I willing to try exercising as part of my recovery process? Because consistency is key, which form of exercise am I most likely to stick with?

Our Experience: The mind, body, and spirit are all connected, and one cannot be balanced without the other two. Start small—the seven-minute workout app is a great way to start.

Prayer: HUGS, please grant me the willingness to consider exercising as part of my road to recovery.

Positive Affirmation: I take care of my mind, body, and spirit.

Words to Live By: "It does not matter how slow you go as long as you do not stop."

THROUGHOUT YOUR DAY
We found that the following has worked for us.

MORNING
Set your intention to exercise today, even if it is only for ten minutes. If you are really crunched for time, the seven-minute workout app is a great solution. Have a plan in place, and always record what you did.

NOON
As you go about your day, make conscious decisions to move and connect with your body. Doing so not only keeps you grounded and centered, but it is also a form of exercise. Walk while tightening your stomach muscles,

take the stairs, and just move your body and connect with it. Those tiny adjustments pay off in the end and are always better than being sedentary.

NIGHT

Notice the difference in the way you feel after a day of having incorporated exercise. If you miss a day, connect with your body through a series of simple stretches. You can access all kinds of exercise-related resources on YouTube.

Other *E* Entries

Etsy: We believe discovering your purpose is one of the greatest tricks to staying recovered. If your purpose is one in which you love to create things and you are looking for an avenue to sell them, try Etsy. The site has a wide range of products including art, photography, clothing, jewelry, and creative knickknacks.

EFT- Emotional Freedom Technique: This technique, also known as energy tapping, is a healing technique that can impact various issues. It may help with anxiety, addiction, phobias, weight control and many other conditions. The principles combine ancient Chinese acupressure and psychology. Tapping with fingers on certain points of the body can produce a calming effect, rewire the brain and balance energy.

Endorphins: Endorphins are the body's natural pain and stress fighters. You can produce more endorphins by regularly exercising, eating healthy, laughing, learning new things, and spending time in nature.

E-Books: We believe it is important to read in recovery. Especially in early recovery, it is essential to carry reading material at all times in order to distract the mind and gain additional insight on your spiritual journey. E-books are an incredible way to be able to read on the go and redirect the mind.

Enlightenment: The journey to enlightenment is similar to having gone through life with a veil in front of your eyes and then having that veil suddenly lifted. To us, enlightenment means having peace regardless of our life situations and surroundings. Being enlightened does not eliminate life's challenges; it shifts your perception to being able to view challenges as lessons and opportunities for growth. It does not change the outer world; it changes a person on the inside. Enlightenment is having an awareness that you can choose peace in any given moment.

Date:

Notes

Date:

Notes

_____

_____

_____

_____

_____

_____

_____

_____

_____

_____

_____

_____

_____

_____

_____

_____

_____

_____

_____

_____

_____

_____

_____

F f

FORGIVE

A CRITICAL COMPONENT to becoming whole and journeying onward to a recovered state is the act of forgiveness. Holding onto anger, resentments, and grudges leads to bitterness and ultimately blocks us from receiving the sunlight of the Holy Spirit. The refusal to forgive stands between you and your higher self and serves no purpose. We must become willing to forgive others, but the most crucial piece to the puzzle here is forgiving yourself. *Nothing* can be accomplished on this path until you forgive yourself for your past. Forgiving unbinds you from your past and ultimately leads directly to healing. In forgiving, you do not forget the past, nor do you condone it. You simply eliminate the negativity that results from holding onto it.

Ask Yourself: Am I willing to forgive myself and others so that I may become whole?

Our Experience: Forgiveness is essential for remaining in a recovered state. Not forgiving will always send you right back to where you came from.

Prayer: HUGS, please grant me the willingness to forgive myself and others for any and all past harms.

Positive Affirmation: The past is gone. I live only in this precious, present moment.

Words to Live By: "The weak can never forgive. Forgiveness is an attribute of the strong." —Mahatma Gandhi

THROUGHOUT YOUR DAY
We found that the following has worked for us.

MORNING

Set your intention to accept that the past has occurred and that it cannot be altered. Let it go, and let it be. If it continues to creep up on you and in your thoughts, pray it away by asking your HUGS to heal you from this pain and redirect your thinking. You may also prefer to meditate on a simple white light.

NOON

Acknowledge the growth you have experienced as a result of the past. Look back and see how far you have come. Always remember that the valleys of our life often lead us to our most amazing blessings and can lead us to our life's purpose.

NIGHT

Express gratitude for the growth you have experienced as a result of the past. Continue to set new goals and new intentions to further this growth. You will see this just comes as a natural progression as you begin to shed layers of your old self.

Other *F* Entries

Family, Fellowship, and Friends: Family is extremely important to those of us in recovery. The support of one's family is crucial and will never be forgotten by those in need. However, there are times during early recovery when your family will not be able to give you the support you need. It is important to note that "family" doesn't necessarily mean a blood relation. In recovery, fellowship and a support network are the foundation of your life. Find your tribe, and stick with them. Lean on them and depend on them when you need to. Find people with similar goals and values, and surround yourself with positive people. It is also acceptable and necessary to eliminate negativity and negative people from your life as well. The people you surround yourself with are a critical component of success in recovery. At the start of your journey, the fellowship or support group will have your back until you develop a true connection with your HUGS.

Date:

Notes

_____

_____

_____

_____

_____

_____

_____

_____

_____

_____

_____

_____

_____

_____

_____

_____

_____

_____

_____

_____

_____

_____

_____

_____

Date:

Notes

G g

GRATITUDE

GRATITUDE IS A critical element in recovery. Gratitude itself is a positive emotion of great importance. It is a deep appreciation that produces feelings of positivity. Simply giving thanks can improve a person's life exponentially. By being grateful, you attract more success, happiness, and emotional wealth into your life. There is always something to be thankful for, and we suggest that each day you make it your mission to find it! Instead of criticizing, overanalyzing, and living in a state of fear, express gratitude for what is going right. Most importantly, when you are faced with a major challenge or tragedy in life, be grateful for it. It is there for your spiritual growth and development. If you are reading this, you have survived 100 percent of your worst days, and your best is yet to come if you are open enough to receive it. And always remember this: life is better when you remain focused on what you do have rather than on what you don't have. Life is so beautiful when you practice gratitude on a daily basis.

Ask Yourself: Am I willing to consider living my days with more gratitude and trying to look for the good even when things are not exactly as I would like them to be?

Our Experience: Gratitude will improve your overall state of wellbeing and will have a very positive effect on your attitude as well.

Prayer: HUGS, allow me the willingness to be grateful for all I have.

Positive Affirmation: I live my life in an intense state of gratitude.

Words to Live By: "Gratitude unlocks the fullness of life." —Melody Beattie

THROUGHOUT YOUR DAY
We found that the following has worked for us.

MORNING
Set your intention to be grateful for the day. Once again, writing in a journal would be a great way to start the day.

NOON
Make a list of everything you are thankful for. This can be as simple as seeing the sun rise in the morning. Gratitude lists can be done daily, weekly, monthly, and yearly.

NIGHT

Have a nightly gratitude session. Take a few minutes to sit and reflect on what you are grateful for each night before going to bed.

Other *G* Entries

Give It Away: Once you enter into a recovered state, to keep it, you have to give it away. It is important to always be sharing the gifts you have received and your experiences with others. Remember, helping them will help you.

Good Orderly Direction (GOD): This is a popular acronym in the recovery community. GOD is used for people who say they do not believe in God or a higher power. That's fine; we still have something for you. Just believe in Good Orderly Direction or in simply doing the next right thing or going in the right direction. You can also simply believe in the power of your support network.

Date:

Notes

_____

_____

_____

_____

_____

_____

_____

_____

_____

_____

_____

_____

_____

_____

_____

_____

_____

_____

_____

_____

_____

_____

_____

_____

Date:

Notes

H h

HIGHER POWER
HUGS
(Higher power, universe, God, spirit)

THE MOST BEAUTIFUL part of being on a spiritual path in recovery is that we get to build our own conception of a higher power. You get to find what we at Starfish Recovery call your HUGS. This definition of our own conception of something greater than ourselves lies at the core of our recovery. You choose to believe in something, anything, that gives you courage, strength, and hope. Some people choose nature, some choose the power of their support network, some choose to believe in the interconnectedness of all living things, and some continue to deepen their understanding of the religion or God they grew up with. Whatever you choose to believe in, it will be personal to you and will give you something to hold onto.

Ask Yourself: Am I ready and willing to consider that there is something bigger than me?

Our Experience: A small amount of willingness will open allow for an open line of communication with a higher power, and your conception of it will evolve and change throughout your journey.

Prayer: HUGS, please grant me the strength and courage to consider that there is something bigger than myself, and help me cultivate my own conception of it.

Positive Affirmation: I surrender to the idea that there is something bigger than me. I will find my HUGS and surrender to its will.

Words to Live By: "My trust in a higher power that wants me to survive and have love in my life is what keeps me moving forward." —Kenny Loggins

THROUGHOUT YOUR DAY
We found that the following has worked for us.

MORNING

Set your intention to be mindful and to live the day in the moment. We find our higher power in the moment. In fact, that is the only place it lives.

NOON

Remember that you are not alone. The more time you spend alone, the less alone you will feel.

NIGHT

Sit quietly before bed, and attempt to quiet your mind and just be. The present moment is the only place you will be able to connect with your HUGS.

Other *H* Entries

Hobbies: Many people in recovery, especially those recovering from addiction, have either lost interest in their hobbies or were just not able to perform them. Discovering new hobbies and rediscovering old ones are great ways to reconnect with your authentic self, discover your purpose, and busy the mind in a positive way.

Holistic: "Holistic" simply means *whole*. We believe recovery treatment must include a holistic approach. Ultimately, this is a journey to wholeness, so whatever types of recovery methods you use, be sure you are treating the mind, body, and soul.

Ho'oponopono: This ancient Hawaiian practice of forgiveness can help restore peace within yourself and with others. This practice consists of repeating the words, "I am sorry. Please forgive me. Thank you. I love you." When you repeat this mantra in connection with a difficult situation or person in your life, you are sending a positive and healing message into the universe. You will begin to heal while restoring your inner harmony.

HUGS Wink: Some people think getting winks from your HUGS is nothing more than coincidence. We believe these winks are signs from your HUGS. They are your HUGS letting you know that you are never alone. HUGS winks are those times when something good or special happens and it just feels like your HUGS caused it. It's when you're down and your HUGS sends you a sign just at the right time to lift you up. HUGS winks show up in the form of numbers, people, animals, symbols, or events. They let you know you are on the right track and to continue following your intuition. It is our experience that once you are open to winks from your HUGS, you will see them all the time.

Date:

Notes

_____

_____

_____

_____

_____

_____

_____

_____

_____

_____

_____

_____

_____

_____

_____

_____

_____

_____

_____

_____

_____

Date:

Notes

_____

_____

_____

_____

_____

_____

_____

_____

_____

_____

_____

_____

_____

_____

_____

_____

_____

_____

_____

_____

_____

_____

I i

INCENSE

INCENSE RELEASES A fragrant smoke when burned, but many people are unaware of its other powers. Incense has always had ties to religious, medicinal, and spiritual aspects of many cultures. It is an essential offering to the gods in many traditions. Incense was suggested in the Bible for use in prayer and meditation; it is believed to welcome in the Holy Spirit and the spirits of our ancestors. The smoke of incense also symbolizes our prayers going up to heaven. Incense can help you to relax, set a tranquil atmosphere, ease anxiety, and make your living space smell amazing. Incense comes in many styles and scents and is very affordable, so you can try a bunch to see which scents you prefer.

Ask Yourself: Am I willing to burn incense and see how it affects my mood and surroundings?

Our Experience: Burning incense enhances our spiritual connection and sets a tranquil mood in our living space. It also helps us to visualize the clearing of old energies and to welcome in the love of our ancestors.

Prayer: HUGS, please grant me the willingness to be open to trying new things and the possibilities of new spiritual experiences.

Positive Affirmation: I am open to trying new things.

Words to Live By: "Light the incense. You must burn to be fragrant." —Rumi

THROUGHOUT YOUR DAY

We found that the following has worked for us.

MORNING

Light incense during your morning prayer and meditation. Invite the Holy Spirit into your space and heart.

NOON

Burn incense in your living space for a calming effect.

NIGHT

Burn incense during evening prayer and meditation. Take note of the various scents you used and any connections you may have made. For example, lemon and pine will energize most people and act as a stimulant, while lavender and sage tends to relax you. A scent such as frankincense will increase your spiritual awareness, and rose will raise your vibration.

Other *I* Entries

Ice cream: Let's face it—ice cream is not just for the kids; we all need a treat now and again. All-natural ice cream actually does provide us with minerals, vitamins, and a burst of energy, and it is obviously delicious. (We do have the cell phone number of our local ice-cream man on hand at all times. Shout out to Mr. Softee!)

Inspiration: Embarking on a spiritual journey will inspire you. As you travel along the road to recovery, you will find your HUGS and your soul's purpose and can begin to bypass all limitations. You come alive and shed what is not really you. Through authentic inspiration, you create a life beyond your wildest dreams.

Instagram: Instagram is a great place to network, find support, get inspiration, and build a community. Instagram can connect you to people around the world who share your common goals and passions. It can also be an amazing tool in starting and growing any new business ideas you may have. We cannot say enough good things about it, as it has connected us to some of the most amazing people in recovery.

Integral Recovery: This is a slightly different approach to addiction and recovery that some may be interested in: www.integralrecoveryinstitute.com.

Intuition: One of the best parts of a spiritual recovery is the intuition you receive. You gain a powerful understanding of the need to listen to your heart. You can literally feel when things aren't right, when someone is being dishonest, or when it is time to remove yourself from a situation. Intuition allows us to fully and completely protect ourselves. With strong intuition, we can eliminate things from our lives before they cause us harm. To us, intuition has become an irreplaceable gift for which we are eternally grateful.

Date:

Notes

Date:

Notes

_____

_____

_____

_____

_____

_____

_____

_____

_____

_____

_____

_____

_____

_____

_____

_____

_____

_____

_____

_____

_____

_____

_____

Jj

JESUS

WE LOVE JESUS, and we're proud of it! We understand that many people are turned off by organized religion, and we respect that and all belief systems. We consider ourselves to be an all-inclusive community and accepting of everyone's beliefs and ideas. We do understand that many people believe that religion often divides people—perhaps you do not know anything at all about the Roman Catholic religion, or perhaps you are indifferent to religion in general. All of these scenarios are fine, but here we want to discuss the person that Jesus Christ was, what he stood for, and how no matter what you believe, he was an extraordinary person to model oneself after. He is unarguably the most recognized figure in history. In recovery, we talk about simply doing the next right thing, and by studying Jesus, we can gain insight as to what that really means. What did Jesus model for us? He modeled forgiveness. He taught us that the Holy Spirit lives in us and that we can and should spread our love and light. He called for peace in all situations and asked us not to sin. He taught us to help others and to recognize evil as a call for love. He taught us to give and to love our enemies. He asked us to pray, to not worry, and to be void of greed. He assured us we should never worry about tomorrow and urged us to care for those in need and those less fortunate. Just trying to live even a little bit like Jesus greatly affects your character, the quality of your life, and the quality of the lives of everyone you come in contact with.

Ask Yourself: Am I willing to consider reading about the life of Jesus and to use his teachings as a guide for simply doing the next right thing?

Our Experience: Jesus Christ is a great person to strive to be like and a powerful example of how one should live as a spiritual being during the course of human life.

Prayer: HUGS, please grant me the willingness to explore the life of Jesus as a possible guide to help me surrender to your will and to provide me with a possible path to a more spiritual way of life.

Positive Affirmation: I will be open to learning new things or looking at things differently.

Words to Live By: What would Jesus do (WWJD)?

THROUGHOUT YOUR DAY
We found that the following has worked for us.

MORNING

Set your intention to do the next right thing and live in the way Jesus would.

NOON

When faced with a difficult situation, we often ask ourselves, "What would Jesus do?"

NIGHT

Consider the ways in which you think you acted as Jesus would throughout the day. Where can you improve? What did you do well?

Other *J* Entries

Jump-rope: Jumping rope is a great way to exercise and relieve stress. It also helps with coordination, balance and focus all things which often need improvement in early recovery.

Date:

Notes

_____

_____

_____

_____

_____

_____

_____

_____

_____

_____

_____

_____

_____

_____

_____

_____

_____

_____

_____

_____

_____

_____

_____

_____

_____

_____

Date:

Notes

K k

KUNDALINI YOGA

KUNDALINI YOGA HAS proven to be a life-changing practice for many people. Kundalini is our latent spiritual energy. It is depicted as a serpent coiled at the base of the spine. The practice of Kundalini yoga awakens this energy. The purpose of the practice is to raise consciousness rising from the chakras (energy centers in the body) to the crown. Eventually, the practice leads us to connection with the infinite and a euphoric state of enlightenment. Yogi Bhajan was the man who gifted authentic Kundalini to the modern world. The Kundalini practice includes a tuning in to the sacred with the chanting of *Ong Namo Guru Dev Namo,* a warm-up, a chosen Kriya meditation, and a savasana (deep relaxation). Over time, this practice is transformative and allows us to tap into the interconnectedness of all living things and, in doing so, to radiate love, light, and peace into the world.

Ask Yourself: Am I willing to consider exploring the practice of Kundalini yoga as a possible addition to my recovery practices?

Our Experience: This practice has improved our lives and also provided us with an easier path to a meditative state.

Prayer: HUGS, grant me the willingness to explore this practice as part of my recovery from life.

Positive Affirmation: I am committed to my Kundalini practice.

Words to Live By: "Remember the entrance to the sanctuary is inside you." —Rumi

THROUGHOUT YOUR DAY
We found that the following has worked for us.

MORNING
Take a Kundalini class, or explore the practice using the Internet.

NOON
As you practice Kundalini, it will automatically carry over into your everyday life; note where and when this has occurred. It will be very slight shifts at first and then more obvious ones as your practice becomes more consistent.

NIGHT
Kundalini yoga uses the mantra *Sat Nam* ("I am truth" or "truth is my name"). Before going to bed, breathe in

Sat and breathe out *Nam.* Repeat this practice multiple times.

For in-depth information on this practice, please visit www.sdkyi.org

Other *K* Entries

Keep It Moving: It is important to be continuously learning and growing in recovery. Recovery from anything requires us to get comfortable with being uncomfortable and to be open to trying new things. We suggest that when you feel stuck, try a new book, a new spiritual practice, or even a new hobby.

Knowledge: When on a spiritual journey, it is better not to intellectualize it too much. However, collect knowledge from as many sources as possible, take what works for you, and leave the rest. As you embark on this journey, you will be handed the exact knowledge that you need at the perfect time—always. As educators, we will always believe knowledge is power!

Kindness: Our overall goal is to leave this world better than we found it. Kindness makes the world a better place. Do the best you can to treat all situations with loving kindness. By thinking of others more and yourself less, you will feel more peace in your heart and mind.

Kirtan: Kirtan is a different kind of music based on an-cient chants. Kirtan has the ability to quiet our minds and bring joy to our spirits. It is a powerful way to meditate. At a Kirtan concert, everyone sings and becomes one voice. Kirtan is commonly referred to as mantra meditation or sacred chanting. Everyone is a part of the music in this very spiritual experience.

Date:

Notes

Date:

Notes

L1

LAUGH

WHEN YOU FIRST enter into the world of recovery, you may think your life as you know it is over, and in many ways, it will be. This is most likely a good thing! You may ask yourself if you will ever have fun and laugh again. We have found more laughter in recovery than one could ever imagine. Don't get us wrong—you will experience pain through your growth, and you will still have bad days and even bad weeks. However, this rebirth is a journey to your higher self. That experience in and of itself is exciting and fun and can be full of laughter. You get to know yourself on a very intimate level—the real you, the you that's been hiding, or the you that has been numbed or buried. You will get to discover your true calling, and in doing so, you will uncover the person you are meant to be. You will come to know what truly makes you laugh, what makes you happy and content, and what gives you a sense of peace. We believe your idea of fun and laughter can entirely change, just as ours did. Now we can't believe all the laughter we missed out on when we were "stuck." Laughter therapy is actually a real practice and can be used to reduce physical and emotional stress, create a happier atmosphere, and improve interpersonal relationships.

Ask Yourself: Am I willing to consider that I can experience fun, humor, and laughter in ways I had never previously imagined?

Our Experience: Today, our concept of fun and laughter is completely different than when we began this journey. And trust us—we are still a good time!

Prayer: HUGS, grant me the willingness to allow new experiences into my life.

Positive Affirmation: I give myself permission to have a new kind of fun and to laugh at myself along the way.

Words to Live By: "Laughter is the best medicine."

THROUGHOUT YOUR DAY
We found that the following has worked for us.

MORNING

Set your intention to do one thing today that makes you feel good and brings a smile to your face. Some things that have worked for us include the following:

Yoga
Reading books that enhance spirituality
Any form of self-care
Meditation

Exercise

Dancing

Recovery meetings

Spending time with family, close friends, and a support group (we guarantee laughter here!)

NOON

Positive thinking plays a huge role. Be open minded and willing to look at activities in a new way of experiencing the new you.

NIGHT

Evaluate how the activity you committed to today made you feel. If it was fun and it made you smile, do it again. If it wasn't enjoyable, try something new tomorrow. This is a chance to explore and learn what your authentic self truly enjoys.

Other *L* Entries

Lapse: We do *not* like the word "relapse," largely because we believe this temporary lapse in your journey can be a huge part of your growth. That being said, when possible, we aim to prevent most slips. We do believe protection from lapses in recovery are possible. Recovery has everything to do with your vibration level. Addiction occurs only when someone is vibrating at a low level. Therefore, in recovery, we are either on an upward or downward swing. The goal is to consistently be vibrating as high as possible. If you are experiencing boredom, worry, jealousy, guilt, or shame, your vibration is lowering, and you are in danger of a slip. On the flip side of the slip is passion, enthusiasm, optimism, and an overall feeling of wellbeing. Those feelings indicate high vibration levels and protection from any potential lapse or slip. Always remember that you are never defined by your relapses but rather by your decision to remain in recovery despite them.

Lavender Oil: We use a lot of lavender oil. We diffuse it, wear it, and breathe it in. It calms the mind and greatly reduces feelings of stress and anxiety.

Learn: We consider ourselves to be lifelong learners. Be willing and ready to learn new things on your path to recovery. Willingness and open-mindedness are two critical components of building the new you. The most successful people are those who are in a constant state of learning new things and ways of being. As Einstein always said, "Be passionately curious."

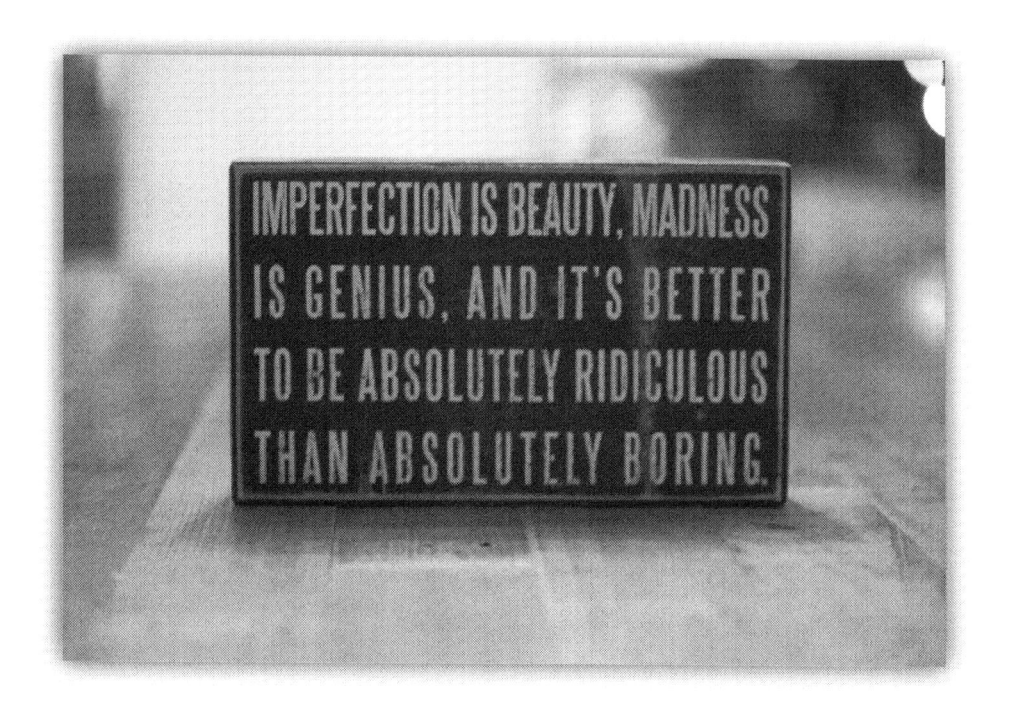

Date:

Notes

Date:

Notes

_____

_____

_____

_____

_____

_____

_____

_____

_____

_____

_____

_____

_____

_____

_____

_____

_____

_____

_____

_____

_____

_____

_____

M m

MEDITATION

IF WE COULD encourage a person in recovery to do one thing and one thing only to improve the quality of his or her life, it would be to meditate. Why? For one thing, it's totally free. Anyone can do it if he or she sticks with it long enough and just keeps trying. It can be used as a coping skill in any situation, anywhere and at any time. It generally creates a sense of joy and wellbeing. For many, it can improve overall happiness. It is the number-one way to listen after praying. But, most importantly, it allows us to tap into our intuition. We all have an inner guide that assists us in discerning which path to take. Any person can learn to tap into this guide, and meditation is the first place to find it. It takes some time to develop this practice, but it is worth the efforts you put in. Do not try to sit for a long period of time at first. As you become connected to your inner guide, this could become the best part of your day. The key here is to just stick with it. The Insight Timer is a great app you can use to allow yourself to be taken through a series of guided meditations, and it also provides many different forms of meditations so that you can try to find one you like best. It also lets you meditate with people from around the world, which is pretty amazing if you stop and think about the power behind that concept.

Ask Yourself: Am I willing to sit quietly for just a few minutes per day in order to begin a practice of meditation?

Our Experience: Meditation has been a key component in our journey to becoming our higher selves and is often one of the highlights of our day. We have found that the more we meditate, the more peaceful and connected we are to our source.

Prayer: HUGS, grant me the willingness to begin a daily meditation practice.

Positive Affirmation: I am committed to my meditation practice.

Words to Live By: "There is a voice that doesn't use words. Listen." —Rumi

THROUGHOUT YOUR DAY
We found that the following has worked for us.

MORNING

After praying, sit quietly for just three minutes and simply listen. Afterward, jot down any ideas or thoughts that came to you.

NOON

Deep breathing, pausing, and slowing down will help you to tap into the intuition that you find during meditation throughout the day.

NIGHT

Prior to going to sleep, once lying comfortably in bed, take a few long, deep breaths. Check in with the way you are feeling in your mind, body, and spirit. Thoughts will come and go, so just let them. The most important thing is that you stay connected here. You will eventually learn how to stay in the moment by quieting your mind. Focusing on your breath or meditating on the silence between sounds may help. Bring yourself to the present moment, and just be. It is always helpful to have paper and a pen on your nightstand. You can even use this book for your notes. Find whatever meditation technique works for you—once again, the key is consistency.

Other *M* Entries

Manifestation: If you can see it, you can have it. Visualize what you want. Put it out into the universe. Pray and meditate on it. Have patience, and keep the faith; it's coming! There are some great books out there on manifesting, or just take a look at the basics behind the laws of attraction.

Massage: There are so many benefits of massages. They are known to reduce stress, pain, and tension. They promote relaxation and can help improve sleep patterns, reduce the effects of chemotherapy, decrease stress, lower blood pressure, and improve cardiovascular health.

Mindfulness: Mindfulness is the art of actually being present in the moment and paying attention to what you are doing. Being mindful can improve every area of your life.

Miracles: They are real. They happen each and every day. If you pray, meditate, and truly believe, you will see.

Music: We listen to a lot of music. Music produces a natural high and can instantly improve your mood. It can also help you to tap into your creative energy and distract you from worries. Music therapy can also be used to address an individual's physical, emotional, cognitive, and social needs.

Date:

Notes

Date:

Notes

N n

NICHIREN BUDDHISM

THE PRACTICE OF Nichiren Buddhism is one that provides us with unlimited access to our true potential. Recovery requires an inner transformation, and Buddhism coincides well with the twelve steps and leads many people on the road to recovery. Participating in the practice has only three requirements: faith, practice, and study. It does not require us to believe or have faith in anything other than our own enlightened Buddha nature. In practicing Nichiren Buddhism, we gain faith because we actually see our quality of life improving. Practice, for us, is chanting *Nam-myoho-renge-kyo* each morning and evening, along with other prayers from the Lotus Sutra in front of a Gohonzon. The study of this practice is easily discovered by seeking out members of Soka Gakkai International, who are always more than willing to share their love of the practice with anyone willing to listen. We have found them to be extremely generous with their time; they have even made frequent visits to our home to acclimate us to the practice, and they have been very patient with our children as well.

Ask Yourself: Am I willing to explore Nichiren Buddhism as a possible addition to my recovery?

Our Experience: This practice has improved our lives and has also provided us with an easier path to a meditative state.

Prayer: HUGS, please grant me the willingness to explore this practice as a part of my recovery from life's challenges.

Positive Affirmation: I am committed to my chanting practice.

Words to Live By: "Whatever your circumstances, whatever your past, the forces that determine your future are nowhere but within your own heart and mind."
—Daisaku Ikeda

THROUGHOUT YOUR DAY
We found that the following has worked for us.

MORNING
As a beginning practice, chant *Nam-myoho-renge-kyo* three times in front of the Gohonzon.

NOON
Chant *Nam-myoho-renge-kyo* whenever you encounter stressful situations or troubling thoughts.

NIGHT

Before going to sleep, chant *Nam-myoho-renge-kyo* three times in front of the Gohonzon.

For more in-depth information on this practice, please visit www.sgi-usa-org.

Other *N* Entries

Nature: Being in nature is one of the best ways to connect to your spirit. It will restore your mental energy, relieve stress, and improve your concentration. It will increase your creativity and improve your overall mental health. Sitting on the ground and feeling the earth beneath you gives you a sense of grounding and rooting that we all need from time to time.

Naturopathic Medicine: This distinct health care treatment uses therapeutic methods and emphasizes prevention to encourage the body's natural self-healing process. It also treats the whole person and focuses on the connection between the mind, body, and soul. You can usually find a naturopathic alternative solution to any ailment, and there are also many health professionals you can seek out to assist you.

Numerology: Numerology is a belief in the divine relationship between numbers and coinciding events. If you like numerology, it can help you to see signs and receive guidance from your HUGS. It can reassure you that you are on the correct path and can provide direction in life.

Nutrition: Nutrition is key in early recovery. You feel better when you eat better—it's as simple as that. Good nutrition can also influence your spiritual awareness. We have found that sticking to a low-sugar, low-carb, and high-protein diet is what keeps us in the best shape and helps us to feel our overall best. (See *D* entry for information on the Daniel Diet.)

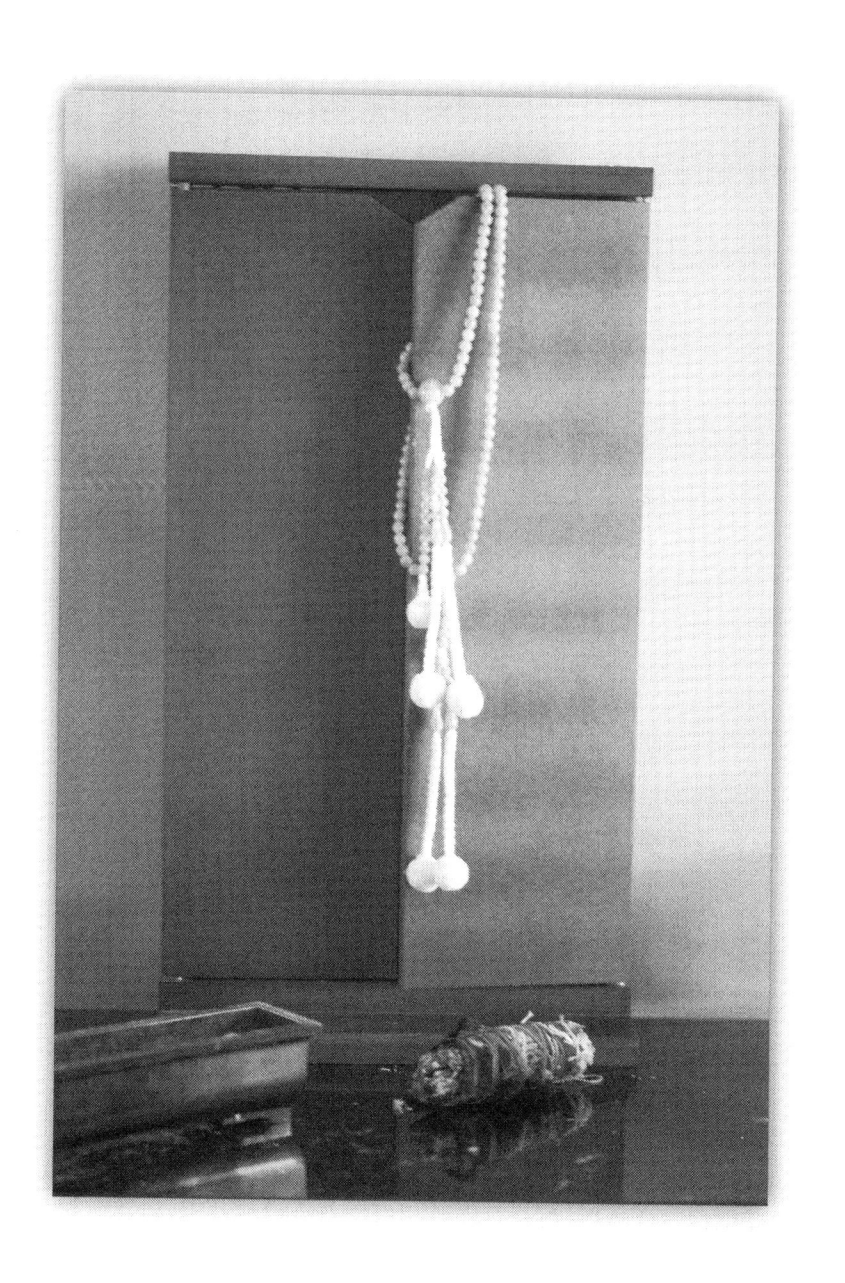

Date:

Notes

Date:

Notes

O o

ORGANIZE

MANY PEOPLE WHO enter into recovery come to the harsh realization that not only were their brains cluttered but that their homes, belongings, and affairs were in disarray as well. Sorting through the disorder can be a daunting and extremely emotional task for most people. By taking the time to organize your surroundings, you will find a sense of peace and comfort in your home. The space around you greatly affects your state of mind as well as your productivity. Neatness, order, organization, and cleanliness produce a feeling of calm, security, and stability. This objective often seems so overwhelming in early recovery, so we suggest taking on small projects at first, such as writing and rewriting lists and prioritizing. There is no better feeling than coming home from a hard day at work to a beautiful space and your very own sanctuary. Some cultures even believe that cleaning up increases good fortune. Why not give it shot?

Ask Yourself: Am I willing to try to organize one aspect of my life?

Our Experience: We have found that being organized is quite simply an easier way to live. When we get stuck in a space for too long, we ask for help.

Prayer: HUGS, please allow me the willingness to organize all areas of my life.

Positive Affirmation: I can organize my life, my mind, and my home.

Words to Live By: "Eliminate physical clutter. More importantly, eliminate spiritual clutter." —D. H. Mondfleur

THROUGHOUT YOUR DAY
We found that the following has worked for us.

MORNING
Begin your day by either reviewing your to-do list or creating a new one. Your list should have daily, weekly, and monthly tasks.

NOON
Check off what has been accomplished, and be sure to prioritize.

NIGHT
Set a new list of goals, and be sure they are reasonable and attainable. Organization is a daily practice, and some

days can set us back. Be easy on yourself, and do the best you can. Tomorrow is a new day.

Suggested reading: *The Life-Changing Magic of Tidying Up* by Marie Kondo

Other *O* Entries

O'M: Daily O'M is an amazing and informative website that features a universal approach to holistic living and focuses on mind, body, and spirit connection. The site offers courses, inspirational messages, horoscopes, and a supportive and uplifting community.

Out of the Dark: Many of us know of the miraculous recovery Gloria Estefan made after a near-fatal accident in 1990. We say *miraculous* because it was nothing short of a miracle. Gloria not only wrote but also performed "Coming out of the Dark" at the 1991 American Music Awards. In recovery, read as many of these inspirational stories as you can until you have the faith in yourself. We all have the ability to find our light and get out of the dark.

Date:

Notes

*This photo was taken at Costa de Este Beach Resort in Vero Beach, Florida. We stumbled upon this hotel because of the lighting and the ambiance. It was our first trip in recovery together and this is where our book really came alive. Unbeknown to us, this hotel was owned by Gloria and Emilio Estefan. There are no coincidences in life.

Date:

Notes

_____

_____

_____

_____

_____

_____

_____

_____

_____

_____

_____

_____

_____

_____

_____

_____

_____

_____

_____

_____

_____

_____

Date:

Notes

P p

PRAY

To PRAY MEANS many different things to many different people. When we suggest prayer, we suggest that you find what praying means to you as an individual and how prayer can help you throughout your day. Many of us live in our ego mind and must learn to shift our thoughts to hear only the voice of our inner guide or spirit. To live mostly in your ego mind is a very lonely, frightening, and often restless place to be. When we open ourselves up to prayer and meditation, we are opening up the gates to our most prized possession—which is our true, authentic self. This is the part of ourselves that we need to find our way back to. This is the part that we may have lost along the way. He or she is still inside you and waiting for you. Prayer can be your "express lane" to rediscovering yourself and developing the deep faith that you will be whole again.

Ask Yourself: Upon awakening, am I willing to start each day with prayer?

Our Experience: The simplest of prayers, when said daily, will lead to the spiritual awakening that you desire.

Prayer: HUGS, grant me the willingness to incorporate prayer into my daily life.

Positive Affirmation: All my thoughts, words, and actions are divinely guided when I pray and stay connected to my source.

Words to Live By: "The fruit of silence is prayer, the fruit of prayer is faith, the fruit of faith is love, the fruit of love is service, the fruit of service is peace." —Blessed St. Mother Teresa of Calcutta

THROUGHOUT YOUR DAY
We found that the following has worked for us.

MORNING
As soon as you open your eyes, ask your higher power—or if you prefer, your higher self—to take over your thinking. Create a quiet spot in your home where you can meet with your HUGS. If you are a newcomer to this practice, an option for beginning a ritual of prayer may be to simply give thanks, as gratitude is key here. Try praying for others. Or simply bring your troubles to your higher self and ask for guidance and direction. Afterward, be sure to sit for a few minutes

in complete and total silence (this is the start of basic meditation—listen).

Noon

Interrupt troubling thoughts by using these prayers: "God, please take over my thinking"; "Spirit, please show me what to do next"; and "Universe, all is well with me, thank you."

Night

Give thanks for another day in recovery! This is also a good time to pray with others via telephone, Facetime, or, if you are lucky enough, in person. When we started this practice, we would reach out to people who we felt had the best connection to their spiritual practice, and we would ask them to pray with us.

Other *P* Entries

Pain: Many people in recovery have spent a great deal of their lives trying to numb their emotional pain. They attempt to avoid feeling all together. However, we should *never* fear pain. Pain is not something to be shunned. It is there for our spiritual growth. Growing through pain is what transforms us into the people our HUGS meant for us to be. The goal is never to be afraid of pain. We say to sit in it, feel it, absorb it, and survive it. It's there to teach you until you have learned the intended lessons, healed the wounds, and experienced true growth. So we say, in terms of pain, walk right into it, face the music, and before you know it, you have learned and the pain is gone.

Peace: Create time and space in each day for complete and total silence. Just *be.* You will experience tremendous growth from this dedication to silence and a sense of peace in your day.

Pilates: This is a great form of exercise that enhances your mental awareness and improves your overall physical wellbeing.

Podcasts: "HOME" is the best!

Positive Thinking: Your thoughts create your reality. The more positive your thoughts, the better your reality. If you are feeling emotional discomfort, there is a very good chance that it is time to take a look at your inner dialogue and the way you are thinking.

Present Moment: Peace and joy are found in the present moment. Live there always! We highly recommend reading *The Power of Now* by Eckhart Tolle.

Date:

Notes

Date:

Notes

_____

_____

_____

_____

_____

_____

_____

_____

_____

_____

_____

_____

_____

_____

_____

_____

_____

_____

_____

_____

_____

_____

_____

Q q

QUIET MIND

It is not easy to cultivate a quiet mind in the world we live in. Technology, work, family, and financial stress offset our natural balance. However, there are ways to be calm on the inside when the world is crazy on the outside. This is a special kind of superpower you can develop in recovery. As we focus on the positive aspects of ourselves and our surroundings, engage in positive self-talk, live in the present, and frequently attempt to reconnect with nature and our HUGS, we can calm our busy minds. Meditation is a key part of cultivating a quiet mind (see *M* entry). It helps to remember that your brain and your mind are two separate entities, and at times they are at odds with one another. Your feelings are not facts; do not waste your time hanging onto the negative ones. Most importantly, there is a ton of power in your breath—use it as often as you need to. A quiet mind will reveal the most beautiful parts of your being...so *shhhhh*.

Ask Yourself: Am I willing to consider that I can be calm and can develop an ability to quiet my mind despite the craziness around me?

Our Experience: Gratitude, being kind to ourselves, self-care, reconnecting with nature and our HUGS, yoga, and meditation have all helped us to commence our days with a quiet mind.

Prayer: HUGS, please allow me the willingness to consider that I can have a quiet mind despite anything that comes my way.

Positive Affirmation: I am quiet. I am calm. My mind is quiet now.

Words to Live By: "Quiet the mind and the soul will speak." —Ma Jaya Sati Bhagavati

THROUGHOUT YOUR DAY

We found that the following has worked for us.

MORNING

Begin your day by sitting quietly for a few minutes in the morning. Thoughts will come and go; it's ok to let them pass. You will start to see that meditation, prayer, breath, and a quiet mind all join together and become part of your daily spiritual practice. You won't have to put much thought into the when, where, and how as they become just a part of your being.

Noon

Repeat your positive affirmation (I am quiet; I am calm; my mind is quiet now).

Night

Attempt repeating the same positive affirmation as you drift off to sleep.

Other *Q* Entries

Queen of Cups Tarot: This intuitive tarot card reader is astoundingly accurate. The Queen of Cups is a beautiful soul who is extremely gifted, intelligent, and generous. This reader has a unique way of interpreting the cards and combines that with her intuition and knowledge of astrology. All hail the Queen!

Quietest Revolution: Amber Khan is a phenomenal spirit. Her readings make you laugh out loud and cry at the same time. Not only is Amber a gifted intuitive and tarot card reader, she has also taught yoga and meditation for over 20 years. Her readings really resonate with many as she focuses on helping her viewers regain their personal power and create resilience after trauma! Check her out!

Quotes: Those of us in recovery send each other a lot of quotes. We read them, write them, and use them to inspire us. Quotes spark discussions, offer insight, give inspiration, and can often encourage someone when he or she is having a bad day.

Date:

Notes

Date:

Notes

R r

READ

READING WHILE ON a spiritual journey is essential. In fact, in line with prayer and meditation, reading and writing are a very close second in terms of importance. You will see that when you pray, you speak to your HUGS; however, when you read, it speaks back to you. Reading books in the genres of self-help, recovery, health, fitness, and, of course, spirituality feeds your conscience and soul while expanding your mind and overall awareness. It also serves an additional purpose by taking us out of our own heads with a healthy distraction and becomes a great coping skill. Reading allows us to engage in something that will build us up and teach us and that can drastically expand our horizons. Entering the world of recovery can be such a beautiful experience when you can find commonalities with people who have gone before you. Reading gives us hope, motivation, and encouragement. You will feel a tremendous amount of gratitude when you realize you have the ability to read, learn new ideas, and focus again.

Ask Yourself: Am I willing to read one simple spiritual book of my own choosing?

Our Experience: Reading has become one of the most important ways we let our HUGS into our minds. It has also served as a useful source and distraction when used as a tool to immediately stop troubling thoughts and to redirect our thinking. It was a comfort on tough days and a friend when no one was around, and it helped us to find our source once again.

Prayer: HUGS, please grant me the willingness to let you in through reading.

Positive Affirmation: Reading is an enjoyable way to let my higher power speak to me.

Words to Live By: "Books were my pass to personal freedom. I learned to read at age three and soon discovered there was a whole world to conquer that went beyond our farm in Mississippi." —Oprah Winfrey

THROUGHOUT YOUR DAY

We found that the following has worked for us.

MORNING

We begin our days with books that provide us with short readings and inspirations for each day of the year.

Examples include *Mornings with the Holy Spirit, Jesus Calling, Jesus and Buddha,* or *Daily Reflections.*

NOON

We always have one spiritual book with us at all times. We read whenever we can. Some of the books that got us started on our journey were the following: *The Power of Now* by Eckhart Tolle; *A Course in Miracles* by Helen Schucman; *The Four Agreements* by Don Miguel Ruiz; *Wisdom of the Ages* by Dr. Wayne Dyer; and *Spirit Junkie* by Gabrielle Bernstein.

NIGHT

We end our days with books that provide us with short readings and inspiration for the close of each day, such as *Evenings with the Holy Spirit.*

Our website, starfishrecovery.com, includes a monthly book review where you may want to begin looking for a book. Remember, your higher power or your inner guide will show you the exact books you need to read.

Other *R* Entries

Reiki: Reiki is a form of Japanese medicine. It promotes healing by working on your life-force energy and in turn improves your overall wellbeing. Visit www.reiki.org for more information, or contact Starfish to be connected to a Reiki master from our community.

Relationships: You can't go it alone on this journey. The universe is all about relationships. Find a group that brings out the best in you. You will discover that once in recovery, you will have the most meaningful and authentic relationships you have ever had.

Retreats: Retreats are a great way to unwind, relax, learn, and connect with others. There are a multitude of retreats out there. Yoga, spiritual, fitness—you name it, there is a retreat for it. Go to retreatfinder.com to find ideas.

Rose Oil: Essential oils are all beneficial in some way; however, rose oil is said to be the queen of all oils and a gift from the angels. It is known to fight depression and anxiety; it can be used as an antiseptic; and it helps women with gynecological disorders. It has various other benefits and is known to naturally raise your vibration. It also has a truly uplifting scent.

Date:

Notes

Date:

Notes

_____

_____

_____

_____

_____

_____

_____

_____

_____

_____

_____

_____

_____

_____

_____

_____

_____

_____

_____

_____

_____

_____

S s

SURRENDER

SURRENDERING TO OUR higher power leads us to our authentic destiny. As humans, we tend to try to control things that are often out of our control. We try to arrange things and make things happen the way we want them to. But the truth is, we don't always know what we need, especially if we are working from our ego or lower power and not our authentic inner guide. When we surrender, we let go and allow things to happen as they are meant to. Most of the time, things always have a way of working themselves out. We don't have to know where we are going or when obstacles are coming, but we must have the faith to know that our higher power will provide for us and that miracles do occur. We don't have to understand why things happen, but we must live with the idea that all events, especially the difficult ones, are meant for our spiritual growth. Just have faith that the universe makes good out of bad, time and time again. This book, our personal stories, and the stories of our Starfish crusaders are living proof of just that.

Ask Yourself: Am I ready and willing to consider there is something bigger than me that I can surrender to and let take the lead?

Our Experience: Everything is always exactly as it is supposed to be. You don't necessarily have to "do" anything, but have faith that all will unfold in divine timing if you are being true to yourself and have a spiritual practice.

Prayer: HUGS, please grant me the willingness to let go of my control issues and turn my will and the direction of my life over to the care of the universe.

Positive Affirmation: I surrender to the idea that there is something bigger than me.

Words to Live By: "Surrender to what is. Let go of what was. Have faith in what will be." —Sonia Ricotti

THROUGHOUT YOUR DAY
We found that the following has worked for us.

MORNING
Set your intention to be mindful and live the day in the moment. We find our HUGS in the present moment. In fact, it is the only place it lives.

Noon

Remember that you are not alone, and the more time you spend alone, the less alone you will feel.

Night

Look closely at your day. See where you tried to control things, and consider how surrendering may have made the situation play out differently. Remember that surrendering is a one-day-at-a-time process. You have to resurrender every day.

Other *S* Entries

Self-Care: Put your oxygen mask on first. If you don't take care of yourself, you cannot help others. Some examples of self-care include exercising, meditating, writing, spending time with supportive friends and family, reading, laughing, manicures, pedicures, and yoga. We could go on forever, but our suggestion is to engage in at least one act of self-care per day that makes you feel good.

She Recovers: Throughout our journey, She Recovers has been an important support network for us. It is a community of women who help others to recover from various struggles. This network is an excellent resource in recovery, and the community retreats are inspiring. The group also offers recovery training and coaching. For more information, check out www.sherecovers.co.

SMART Recovery: SMART Recovery is an international nonprofit organization that provides assistance to individuals seeking abstinence from addictive behaviors. Visit www.smartrecovery.org for more information.

Smudging: Smudging is done with a smudge stick or a bundle of dried herbs (usually sage). Smudging is said to purify a space and clear it of negative energies. Smudging can clear the air, produce a relaxing effect, and increase energy. It can be used as a way to bless your home or prepare your space for spiritual practice. Smudging yourself will also clear any negative emotional or spiritual energy you have hanging around. In essence, you smudge to release what no longer serves you and to invite positive energy into your space and being.

Spirituality: Spirituality is not religion. It is about connecting to your higher self and connecting to something greater than you. It is the interconnectedness of all living things, and to us, it's the key to the universe and life. It is what is at the core of our recovery. It's a universal human experience, and it is something that touches every single living thing.

Spiritual Teacher: Seek out and find a guru in whatever spiritual practice you want to learn. This is life changing! When you learn from the best, it will enhance both the quality and speed of your recovery. Trust us—we know this firsthand.

Solfeggio Frequencies: These are ancient sounds that can be listened to as a form of therapy and meditation in order to improve one's sense of security and love, to release fear and guilt, to bring about change, to heal relationships, and to increase spiritual awareness.

Date:

Notes

Date:

Notes

T t

TIME

PEOPLE OFTEN LOOK at those of us in recovery and ask us how long it will take them to get to a certain point. It is important for people to remember that this is all a process and that there is no such thing as a finished product. We are always in a constant state of evolving, learning, and trying new things, and most importantly, we are assessing ourselves and our behaviors daily. Rather than focusing on time, focus on getting well and becoming whole once again. This means something different depending on the type of recovery you are in. Many people who are in recovery from substance abuse need time to go through the steps, time to work with a sponsor, time to heal, time to make amends, and time to practice this new way of life. In all forms of recovery there is a process, and it is unique to each individual. We should all remember to take this one day at a time. Just know that in each day of recovery, you are learning and growing and ultimately becoming the best version of yourself. Letting go of the idea of time is really one of the most important aspects to recovering from anything. It will be different for all of us. Take it minute by minute at first, be patient and loving with yourself, and trust that if you do the work, time truly does heal all wounds.

Ask Yourself: Am I willing to trust the process and be patient with myself as the road to recovery takes time?

Our Experience: Time will go by faster if you seek out the best spiritual teachers and gurus, surround yourself with positive people, and use the power of prayer to your advantage.

Prayer: HUGS, please allow me the willingness to be patient with myself and trust the process of recovery.

Positive Affirmation: I will be patient with myself and know that time is on my side.

Words to Live By: "Everything heals. Your body heals. Your heart heals. The mind heals. Wounds heal. Your soul repairs itself. Your happiness is always going to come back. Bad times don't last."- Author Unknown

THROUGHOUT YOUR DAY
We found that the following has worked for us.

MORNING
Set your intention to trust the process, and be patient with yourself.

NOON

Choose one thing from this book to do for your recovery today. Focus on it.

NIGHT

Pray for the willingness to continue on this journey, and release the idea of time, as it is truly just an illusion anyway.

Other *T* Entries

Tarot: Some people think it's weird and don't agree with it, but we love tarot. YouTube it, get your own deck, get read by a reputable intuitive card reader, and just have fun with it. We believe it has provided us with guidance and enhanced our intuition and revelation, especially during times we felt stuck or blocked. Tarot can become addicting and used for the wrong reasons, so exercise some caution here. (We suggest that before reading tarot on your own, you should either learn from an experienced professional or do some research. You do not want to invite negative energies in.)

Travel: If you have the funds, see the world. If you don't, set up a travel fund today! Travel brings joy, learning experiences, and an appreciation for other cultures. It also gives you a chance to spread your message of love as a Starfish crusader around the world. Travelling often helps us realize those big problems we thought we had are really quite small.

Toolbox: There will be times when you struggle. Have a toolbox ready. This book has everything you need to start.

Therapy: Get on the couch. It will help. Waking up spiritually is the number-one part of recovery. However, therapy will help you to examine and change unhealthy patterns of behavior. It can also help with healing the inner child that is so often the cause of our struggles.

Date:

Notes

Date:

Notes

U u

UNITY

IN THE WORLD of recovery, fellowship equals unity. A fellowship or a support group refers to the people who come together because of similar life experiences and who then stay together because they practice similar solutions to recover from those experiences. In most cases, and always in twelve-step fellowships, the members share the common belief that a spiritual way of life is the answer to all of life's challenges. Fellowship, especially in the early stages of recovery, is critical to remaining in a recovered state. The unity of the fellowship will have your back until you have a strong connection to your HUGS. A fellowship or a support group will provide you with information and advice, give you emotional and social support, and allow you to build a new network of connections and friends. The people you surround yourself with on this journey are critical to your success. The interaction and unity of the fellowship is a key ingredient to the success of someone's recovery. Fellowships and support groups are not all created equal, and you must seek the one that best suits your recovery needs.

Ask Yourself: Are you willing to accept a fellowship or support group as a critical part of your recovery?

Our Experience: We have made some of the best friends of our lives within the unity of our fellowship.

Prayer: HUGS, allow me the willingness to welcome people and supportive relationships into my life.

Positive Affirmation: I will find my tribe. I will ask for help when I need help.

Words to Live By: "Call it a clan, call it a network, call it a tribe, call it a family, whatever you call it, whoever you are, you need one!" —Jane Howard

THROUGHOUT YOUR DAY
We found that the following has worked for us.

MORNING

Set the intention to make it to a meeting of any fellowship of your choosing at some point in your day, or even weekly or monthly depending on your need.

NOON

Check in with your support group periodically throughout the day. Even if you are having a great day, one of your fellows may not be, and helping him or her will help you as well.

Night

Call or send a text to someone in your network before going to bed. We usually find ourselves in a group text at some point throughout our day. Sharing the good and the bad brings you all together.

Other *U* Entries

Unicorns: Spirituality and unicorns have much in common, as they are something people strive to see and feel, but they remain unseen. In the world of recovery, unicorns symbolize the journey, the sacred quest, to help us find our true core. Unicorns have long been a representation of the moon, a female energy. As the moon reflects the light of the sun, the unicorn reflects the energies at play in our own lives.

Unlock Dreams: We are all born with dreams. The key is to keep your dreams alive. Life gives us all a set of struggles to go through. We must not downsize our dreams as a result of our struggles. Look to your HUGS to unlock your dreams.

Untapped Potential: Once you are in a recovered state and find your HUGS, you will tap into your natural abilities and creative energies and will ultimately find your unlimited potential and your life's purpose.

Date:

Notes

_____

_____

_____

_____

_____

_____

_____

_____

_____

_____

_____

_____

_____

_____

_____

_____

_____

_____

_____

_____

_____

Date:

Notes

V v

VIBRATION

EVERYTHING IN THE universe is energy. Your vibration is your overall state of being. We invite things into our lives with our frequencies, and we will attract what we give off from our mental, physical, spiritual, and emotional energies. By becoming aware of your thoughts, walking in gratitude and sticking to a healthy lifestyle, you can actually raise your vibration and positive energies. Meditation, prayer, kindness, exercise, and helping others are all simple ways to raise your vibration, improve your overall wellbeing, and ultimately attract what you want into your life. Hard alcohol, mood-altering substances, junk food, toxic relationships, excessive amounts of red meat, medications, negative feelings and emotions, and, most importantly, negative thoughts—do your very best to steer clear of those, and focus instead on deep-breathing techniques, yoga, laughing, relaxing music, being in nature, grounding, and even something as simple as smiling.

Ask Yourself: Am I willing to try some simple steps ways to raise my vibration?

Our Experience: When the suggestions above are used regularly, you begin to attract positive things, people, and situations into your life. Others may think you are having a streak of good luck, but it is really your energy manifesting what you truly desire.

Prayer: HUGS, allow me the willingness to try some new ways to raise my vibration and overall wellbeing.

Positive Affirmation: All the positive energies of the universe are flowing through me.

Words to Live By: "Everything that you are living is a literal translation of the vibration you have been offering." —Abraham Hicks

THROUGHOUT YOUR DAY

We found that the following has worked for us.

MORNING
Starting your day with prayer and meditation connects you to your HUGS and instantly raises your vibration.

NOON
Be sure to go through your day expressing gratitude and practicing loving kindness. Also be sure to stay hydrated and fuel your body with healthy foods.

Night

Before bed, reflect on the positive parts of your day, and always strive to make the next day a little better.

Other *V* Entries

Valerian Root: This is a natural herb that is known to ease insomnia and anxiety and produce an overall calming effect.

Vision Board: A vision board is the creation of a sacred space that displays, through the use of pictures, photos, and quotes, your true heart's desires. When you create this board, be sure to place it in a spot where you will see it often. By creating and looking at your board, you are actually doing visualization exercises. Visualization sends a powerful frequency out into the universe and allows you to ultimately manifest what you want through seeing it.

Vitamins: Vitamins can prevent and treat various diseases. They help with important bodily functions, such as metabolism, immunity, and digestion.

Date:

Notes

_____

_____

_____

_____

_____

_____

_____

_____

_____

_____

_____

_____

_____

_____

_____

_____

_____

_____

_____

_____

_____

Date:

Notes

W w

WOUND WORK
(Healing Ancestral Wounds)

YOUR LIFE IS a result of the choices made by those who came before you. There is a belief that comes from the Native Americans in which it is said that our actions affect seven generations before us and seven generations after us. They believe that we can evolve our ancestral lineage not only going forward but backward as well. If there is one thing that both science and religion can agree on, it is that we are all energy. The energy that embodied your ancestors was passed on to you, and your energy will be passed on to those who come after. Therefore, as you transform, the energy of your ancestors is also transformed. This is where wound work comes in. As you heal your wounds, you can heal the wounds for your entire lineage. You can practice forgiveness, change and teach new beliefs, feel pain and heal yourself from it, and let go of hurt that has followed your lineage for generations. Simply put, as you heal, so do those who have passed. You can bring them to wholeness and set up what happens for future generations. You can ignore this energy if you want, but you will never break the cycle. Addiction is a place where this example can be illustrated best. Perhaps within your lineage there is a history of substance abuse. This is carried down from generation to generation because those who suffered from addiction were not taught how to heal. You can change this. As you do your wound work you will heal, you will heal the generations to come, and, in doing so, you will break the ancestral cycle of something as insidious as addiction. Regardless of your individual ancestral patterns, you do have the power to break them. You can heal your wounds and become the light. It takes courage to look within and heal, but it can be done. When you make a conscious effort to heal yourself, you are making peace with the past and changing the future for all generations to come.

Ask Yourself: Am I willing to consider that I am important enough to be the light for my entire lineage?

Our Experience: Healing ourselves has broken the cycle of negative patterns that have existed in our families for many generations. Our children are being taught a different way of living as a direct result of our wound work and healing.

Prayer: HUGS, please allow me the willingness to heal my wounds so that I may help others.

Positive Affirmation: My wound work will allow me to heal my entire lineage.

Words to Live By: "Every woman that heals herself helps heal all the women who came before her, and all those who came after her." —Christine Northrup

THROUGHOUT YOUR DAY
We found that the following has worked for us.

MORNING

Choose one thing today that you believe you need to let go of. Ask your HUGS to help you let go of it. As it pops in your head throughout the day, consciously ask your HUGS to redirect your thinking.

NOON

Allow yourself to feel the pain of whatever you must let go of. Do not become numb to it; just be with the pain, and ask your HUGS to heal you from the wound. Let it go. It is important to stay away from a victim mentality. Healing requires looking only at yourself. Throughout the day, focus on the present.

NIGHT

Talk to your HUGS about forgiveness, letting go, and healing from whatever wound you are currently focusing on healing.

Other *W* Entries

Walks: Walking can help maintain a healthy weight and prevent and manage various health conditions. It can strengthen the body and provide relief from anxiety in the earliest days of recovery. It also reduces stress and provides you with time to decompress. Walking in nature can prove to be even more beneficial. This is a great activity that can be done anytime with anyone.

Walking Labyrinth: Walking the labyrinth will foster peace and tranquility while providing you with a low-impact exercise. They can be sacred spots for walking meditation and a place to set and manifest intentions.

Worship: The art of worship toward a higher power is not what many people think it to be. True worship is bringing pleasure to something greater than yourself. We do this by trusting that there is something greater than us and having faith that that power can and will always provide for us. Becoming best friends with your own concept of a higher power of your personal understanding or finding your HUGS is the best way to live. Actually, it is the only way to live in peace and tranquility despite your circumstances, situations, feelings, and emotions. Shifting to an attitude of surrender and worship to your HUGS is the most liberating, amazing life change one can ever experience. We no longer control our lives, and in doing so, we become a far more amazing version of ourselves because it's the most liberating, amazing life change one can ever experience. We no longer control our lives, and in doing so, we become a far more amazing version of ourselves because it's the authentic self that God created us to be. Most people hear this and truly don't understand, but with practice, this enlightenment is easily accomplished. Worship does not mean sitting in prayer and reading the Bible all day long. It is more like a constant conversation with your HUGS. It's including your HUGS in your everyday routines. It's almost like we practice the presence of a higher power at all times. It's a perpetual attitude and belief of the fact that you are always being guided and trusting the intuition you receive from this guide.

Date:

Notes

Date:

Notes

_____

_____

_____

_____

_____

_____

_____

_____

_____

_____

_____

_____

_____

_____

_____

_____

_____

_____

_____

_____

_____

_____

_____

_____

X x

X-AMINE
Self-Examination

WHAT OFTEN LIES within many people who have experienced trauma at a young age is what we like to call their "haunted house." A haunted house is a place inside a person where he or she has never dared to enter. Very often the memories of these events are too painful to process, and people turn to substances or other unhealthy addictions to block or numb them. The memories of these wounds can surface or come to light as one enters into recovery and his or her brain begins to heal. This can be referred to as PTSD, or post traumatic stress disorder. Through the process of uncovering, we discover that our addictions are nothing more than a mere symptom. Our mind, or our haunted house, is the problem.

Ask Yourself: Am I ready and willing to open the door to my haunted house and closely examine my inner child, thoughts, patterns, and beliefs?

Our Experience: This is a very personal choice and needs to be handled delicately. It is an inside job. When you become brave enough and are willing to look deeply inward and engage in this type of self-examination, it is truly a life-altering experience. Many of us at this juncture will need to ask for professional help to truly open the doors of the haunted house and gain access to our highest self. Doing so with a trusted friend, therapist, sponsor, or clergy will help to crack the haunted house open, and this is where true growth occurs. Clearly, this is a slow process and is not to be completed in a twenty-four-hour period. However, small things can be done each day that will help you to press on and clean out your haunted house and honestly examine your inner being. This is the only way healing can occur.

Prayer: HUGS, please grant me the strength and courage to walk into my haunted house, face my pain, and set myself free once and for all.

Positive Affirmation: My heart is open. I allow the universe to guide me through my thoughts and toward healing so that I may feel peace in my heart once again.

Words to Live By: "If it's challenging you, testing you and pushing you...it's helping you become more of who you're meant to be." —Mandy Hale

THROUGHOUT YOUR DAY
We found the following has worked for us.

MORNING

Set the intention to keep the focus on yourself. In your morning prayers (see *P* entry), ask your HUGS to show you the parts of you that remain unhealed and to lead you to people and situations that will allow the process of healing to take place.

NOON

Repeat your positive affirmation.

NIGHT

Ask your HUGS to grant you the willingness to look inward and to continue to grow spiritually.

Date:

Notes

Date:

Notes

_____

_____

_____

_____

_____

_____

_____

_____

_____

_____

_____

_____

_____

_____

_____

_____

_____

_____

_____

_____

_____

_____

_____

Y y

YOGA

YOGA IS AN essential part of our recovery and one that we wish to share with as many people as possible. Yoga is a group of physical, mental, and spiritual practices that originated in the Eastern world. In Sanskrit, *yoga* literally means to "join or unite." The mind, body, and soul are never separate. All three must be joined and working together for a person to experience wholeness. A habitual yoga practice exponentially increases the quality of this union. There are many forms of yoga. Bikram, Anusara, Ashtanga, Hatha, Vinyasa, and Kripalu are just a few of the more popular forms. People in the beginning stages of recovery should definitely try restorative yoga, as it is known to be extremely relaxing and simple to follow. The trick is to find the style that connects with your purpose, personality, or need at any given time. We found that we connected best with Kundalini (see *K* entry), but we are open to and often practice various styles of yoga. All forms of yoga really have one goal in mind: a healthy mind, body, and soul that work together to help you peacefully navigate your way through life's ups and downs.

Ask Yourself: Am I willing to try different forms of yoga?

Our Experience: After trying different forms, we fell in love with Kundalini, and it has proven to transform our minds, bodies, and souls. We used YouTube a lot in the beginning to save on costs until we were committed to a particular practice.

Prayer: HUGS, allow me the willingness to try different types of yoga as part of my recovery.

Positive Affirmation: I am committed to my daily yoga practice.

Words to Live By: "Yoga is not about touching your toes; it's about what you learn on the way down." —Jigar Gor

THROUGHOUT YOUR DAY
We found that the following has worked for us.

MORNING
Set your intention to try just three yoga poses that day. You can look up the basic postures online.

NOON
On your lunch break, roll out a mat, take your shoes off, and practice again.

NIGHT

Try three additional postures from the form of yoga you chose. Commit to doing three postures a day for two weeks. See what happens!

Other *Y* Entries

YouTube: If Money is an issue in your recovery, YouTube is the place to go. You can learn how to utilize any entry in this book through the use of YouTube.

Date:

Notes

Date:

Notes

_____

_____

_____

_____

_____

_____

_____

_____

_____

_____

_____

_____

_____

_____

_____

_____

_____

_____

_____

_____

_____

_____

Z z

ZIG ZAG TO RECOVERY

WE END WITH this entry because this belief will bring comfort to anyone looking for a path for recovery. In fact, this is probably one of the most important ideas to consider in all of our work. We believe that there is no straight line to recovery. There is no one path. We are all unique, and the same program, technique, philosophy, or idea will not work for everyone. In recovery you may have to turn left, then abruptly turn right, then left again, and then head straight. We just don't know. The trick is to zigzag from one thing to the next and pick up what works for you along the way. For us, a twelve-step program was a start, but it was not enough, and it did not lead us to our purpose. It began the journey, but there had to be more. We zigzag through recovery, trying a little bit of everything, and we hold onto what feels like it fits, the things that make us feel whole and childlike—and we leave the rest. This is how we became and stay recovered; this zigzag to recovery is what ultimately leads you to your purpose. It's how we found out who we are, and most of all, it's how we learned that recovery is a lifelong process of learning, creating, growing, evolving, believing, and exploring—one day at a time.

Ask Yourself: Am I willing to consider a zigzag to recovery until I find a path that works for me?

Our Experience: No one path to recovery should be set in stone. You need to take what works for you and leads you to feeling the most connected to your highest self.

Prayer: HUGS, show me the path that you know is best for me.

Positive Affirmation: I will be open to finding my own way.

Words to Live By: "Why fit in when you were born to stand out?" —Dr. Seuss

THROUGHOUT YOUR DAY
We found that the following has worked for us.

MORNING

Look through our glossary and choose one thing that sparks your interest to focus on today.

NOON

Use this idea technique or strategy throughout the day.

NIGHT

Evaluate how you felt when you did focus on a particular entry If it feels natural, the time flies, and you feel at peace when doing it, use it again. It is a natural part of your journey that you should continue to use as much as possible.

Date:

Notes

Date:

Notes

People, Prayers, Products and Paperbacks that lead us to our HUGS ......

<u>Paperbacks</u>
Eckhart Tolle
The Power of Now
A New Earth

Scribed by Helen Schucman
A Course in Miracles

Gabrielle Bernstein
May Cause Miracles
The Universe Has Your Back
Spirit Junkie

Rick Warren
The Purpose Driven Life

Dr. Wayne Dyer
Wisdom of the Ages

Don Miguel Ruiz
The Four Agreements

People

Dawn Nickel
Taryn Strong
Gabrielle Bernstein
Marianne Williamson
Corrina DiLeo
Glennon Doyle Melton
Scott Stabile
Oprah Winfrey - SuperSoul Sunday

Prayers

The Serenity Prayer
God, Grant me the serenity
to accept the things I cannot change,
The courage to change the things I can
and the wisdom to know the difference.

The Set Aside Prayer:
"Dear God please help me to set aside everything I
think I know about [people. place or thing] so I may
have an open mind and a new experience. Please help
me to see the truth about [people. place or thing].
AMEN." (This prayer comes from the Big Book of AA).

Third Step Prayer:

"God, I offer myself to thee - to build with me and do with
me as Thou wilt. Relieve me of the bondage of self, that
I may better do Thy will. Take away my difficulties, that
victory over them may bear witness to those I would help
of Thy Power, Thy Love and Thy Way of life. May I do Thy
will always!"(This prayer comes from the Big Book of AA).

A prayer of St. Francis of Assisi:

"Lord, make me an instrument of your peace; where
there is hatred, let me sow love; where there is injury,
pardon; where there is discord, union; where there
is doubt, faith; where there is despair, hope; where
there is darkness, light; and where there is sadness,
joy.
"O Divine Master, grant that I may not so much seek to
be consoled, as to console; to be understood, as to understand; to be loved, as to love; for it is in giving that
we receive, it is in pardoning that we are pardoned,
and it is in dying that we are born to eternal life."
Amen.

Come Holy Spirit Prayer:

Come Holy Spirit, fill the hearts of your faithful and
kindle in them the fire of your love. Send forth your

Spirit and they shall be created. And You shall renew the face of the earth.

O, God, who by the light of the Holy Spirit, did instruct the hearts of the faithful, grant that by the same Holy Spirit we may be truly wise and ever enjoy His consolations, Through Christ Our Lord, Amen.

Prayer to your HUGS
HUGS, may thy will be done, always.

<u>Products</u>
The following is a list of products by a company that brought us closer to our HUGS and continues to help us on our journeys. Please explore the products below and use the accompanying **link and code** to make purchases.

IZZY BELL
Aromatherapy Jewelry

Get 15% off any aromatherapy jewelry by entering in coupon code:
Starfish at checkout
website: www.izzybelljewelry.com

Izzybell Jewelry started as two busy moms who loved the benefits of Aromatherapy and loved the look of fashion and set out to merge both together in a fun way. They specialize in functional, fashionable jewelry and infuse each piece with positive affirmations before the packaging process. We LOVE them because their philosophy is similar to ours. They inspire, give back and hope to make the world a better place.

Our Izzy Bell Favorites:

Starfish Pendant - STARFISH pendant... enough said right? This essential oil diffuser necklace is a pendant and provides a place to dab essential oils for soothing aromatherapy benefits.

Essential Oil Diffuser 5 Stone Lava Rock Wrap Bracelet
We love the Lava Bracelet. It's stylish, uplifting and the lava is known to help with concentration. We love to couple this with our favorite essential oil and breathe in as needed.

Essential Oil Diffuser Wristband Enjoy the soothing benefits of aromatherapy with this essential oil diffuser wristband that includes five absorbent inserts that diffuse the scent of your favorite essential oils. Velcro band and adjusts for smaller or larger wrist sizes and works great for adults and children.

Turquoise Stone Brown Leather Bracelet
This essential oil diffuser bracelet features beautiful leather, a pop of turquoise, and an easy-to-open locket to hold your essential oils as you go about your day. It's the perfect accessory to any outfit, and will enhance your mood through the power of essential oils!

Boho Black Leather Essential Oil Diffuser Bracelet
Wear, smell and enjoy your favorite essential oils in style with this brown leather aromatherapy diffuser bracelet with adjustable rope band. This essential oil diffuser bracelet features an easy to open locket to apply your favorite essential oil.

ABOUT THE AUTHORS

TRICIA RAGUSA IS a mother of four and a secondary educator with a passion for passing knowledge onto others. Tricia lives a spiritual life and wishes to share her experiences with anyone recovering from any trauma.

Michele Leigh Dionisio is an elementary school teacher and mother of twin girls who has devoted her life to nurturing our youth. Michele lives a life beyond her wildest dreams and wishes to share her hope with anyone looking to live their best life.

They believe there are various ways to recover beyond the typical rhetoric. They discuss a Zig Zag to recovery in which people are encouraged to use any means possible to live a full life and ultimately discover their life's purpose.

All photos are compliments of Eternal Glo Photography, LLC and shot by Michele Leigh Dionisio herself. The items photographed in this book are mostly personal items with significant meaning to the authors. The shooting of the photographs are an important part of Michele's journey as it was the first time she picked up her camera since entering recovery in 2016.

Made in the USA
Lexington, KY
20 February 2018